Right On Time

A collection of poems by Donnel Davis

W0115566

Table of contents

First and foremost, I want to give praise to Jesus Christ for blessing me with the opportunity to share my gift with the world. I'm only able to accomplish this dream because of you and the loving people that you have surrounded me with.

I would also like to thank my parents, the two people who have been there for me from the very beginning. When I made poor decisions and succumbed to the ways of the world, they never turned their backs on me.

I want to give special thanks to my wife, my soul mate, and my best friend, Michelle. Thank you for your loyalty, for your support, and for pushing me to move forward. I have given you more than a fair share of headaches and restless nights, but we're on our way.

I also want to give a special thanks to my sister, Kim: my brothers Brandon, Tremain, Los,4, BJ, Grace (LL), Dj Screw (LL): Granny: my Grace Congregational Church family, and my two beautiful princesses Sydney and Cameron for being patient with me as I stepped into a new role. I'm doing this to glorify God, provide inspiration for others, and provide a better life for us. Much love to all the other family members and friends.

Right On Time

Pummeled by persecution, but I'm still here

Delinquency notices decorated the front door of my apartment, but I'm still here

Fear of becoming a failure funneled through my feeble frame and fueled my drive

No lights, no running water, and continuous hunger pains couldn't and wouldn't kill my vibe

I survived, I'm alive, now I'm striving for a better life

Anything worthwhile comes at a hefty price

Sacrifice, dedication, and determination are imperative for success

Hurdles are inevitable but they will not impede my progress

Blessings come from above at the most opportune times

The darkness has been erased and replaced with nothing but sunshine

My time is now, but God deserves all the glory

I followed the light and pursued my dreams, now the world is able to witness my story

4

True Freedom

The sirens wailed and were followed by a sea of lights

More than an hour ago, another young man lost his life

A continuous plight spurned by a senseless act

Tears streamed down her face, she knew her son would not be coming back

No weapons, no drugs were found yet he was accosted and slain

Will justice surface or will the power of the badge continue to reign?

Pain supersedes our better judgement and we ignite more pain

Before the eye of the public, dreams burst into vacuous flames

So, let's educate the youth: they are future doctors, lawyers, and teachers

Some will entertain us, some will be preachers

So, let's band together and extend our hearts to those in need

True freedom is obtainable as long as we follow God's lead

Drowning In Sin

His arms flailed and he kicked his legs with all his might

But currents raged like a caged beast and now he was in a fight for his life

The elements were just too much for him to bear alone

He saw his father take his breath and his mother sacrificed her body to keep the lights on

The place he called home was weathered and riddled with violence

He was entrapped in turmoil and he found solace in remaining silent

Survival initiated criminal thinking

Greed and lustful ways had him sinking

Further and further into a pool of sin

The devil looked on with an impish grin

But God was with him all along

He was waiting and waiting to be called upon

He was fully submerged when he cried out

"Jesus, Jesus, please save me, you are my only way out"

Within minutes, he was back on dry land

We must humble ourselves and be fully submissive because God always has a plan

Emancipation

His posture was porous and his clothes were tattered

His stride was fragmented and his hair was matted

He acknowledged the frowning faces with a simple nod

If only they knew that they were in the presence of a God

He adjusted the microphone to his liking before he let out an exaggerated sigh

The smirks were replaced with anxiety when they saw the fire in his eyes

He was alive, his words painted a picture for the ages

His mastery and the energy that he generated were ultra-contagious

Cages were pried open and dreams became reality

Birds soared beyond the skies and troops rejoined their cavalry

The totality of his performance was well-deserving of a standing ovation

Although he was financially challenged, this was his emancipation

Proceed

Immunity from adversity is fictious

Opportunities will surface so I remain ambitious

Embedded in the trenches, but I envision victory

Witnesses understand my mannerism, but to others it remains a mystery

Initially overlooked, now I'm the brain behind a budding brand

Concrete jungles have been replaced with bohemian blue waters accented with white sand

Here I stand today, a man with an acute sense of direction

Naysayers will conspire against me, but the Lord is my protection

No need for an election, I've been chosen to lead

My savior's resume is flawless, so I proceed with the utmost belief

Misery Lane

Broken hearts and shattered dreams are my neighbors

So who can I turn to when I'm in need of a favor

Money is scarce, but problems are prevalent

Souls are sold for pennies in an attempt to regain relevance

Negligence is a fad that won't subside

And jealousy is like a virus that just won't die

Bullets fly like baby birds and create calamity

Consequences arrive and killers plead insanity

Some families escape and never look back

While others promote change but they just can't stay on track

We are under attack, but a lot of it is self-inflicted

The answer is only a prayer away: so humble yourself, follow the Spirit, and cash in your ticket

Owning The Moment

A cacophony of boos rained from the rafters

His heart rapped against his chest plate as he swayed on the scaffold

Anxiety boiled in his belly but this was the stage, his moment

Repetition piqued his confidence, now he was ready to own it

This was more than a performance-this would be a tantalizing testimony

The faces were those of strangers, but the elements ensured that he would not be lonely

The matrimony between him and his thoughts were simply seamless

His strides were so powerful and graceful that he birthed more dreamers

His fingers knifed through the wind with no resistance

Even his pigmentation couldn't overshadow how he obliterated the competition

Tears of joy welled in his eyes as he looked toward the sky

A gift from God and dedication ensured that he would not be denied

Don't Park Here

Complacency is detrimental to your mission

Commitment with no passion is like after school detention

Proximity is an attraction but it shouldn't be a closer

Life is a journey so prepare yourself like a soldier

Self appraisal is essential

Fame and glamor are cool benefits but seek knowledge and utilize your wisdom

Potential is a vehicle that can only carry you so far

Vacancies will appear but don't park your car

Visit and try on the clothing but avoid selling out

Calculate your steps and survey your route

Erase doubt by following the light that God has provided for you

Follow the narrow road and you will be rewarded with an envious view

One Day

Lush, green lawns trace this magnificent estate

Perfectly positioned balconies provide a picturesque view of a sunbathed lake

Birds chirp in perfect harmony and create a soundtrack for this serene setting

Partygoers don pristine garments as if this were a royal wedding

Flasks overflow with expensive champagne

Conversations range from favorite entertainers to upcoming campaigns

Far from mundane, this is the hottest ticket in town

Invitations only, everybody is adorned with a bejeweled crown

Frowns are nonexistent, smiles are everywhere

Revelers grace the dance floor and laughter permeates the air

But a familiar sound interrupts his imagination and it's back to reality

Hopefully one day, his thoughts and his dreams can become his true reality

Salvation

Calloused hearts and severed souls carousel through life probing for a purpose

I envision salvation while most deem them worthless

So I channel my knowledge and extend my hand

Only through God's grace was I provided a second chance

Grand opportunities await us such as streets made of gold and eternal living

Improved conditions do not mean that we're no longer in prison

Become a witness and you shall see the light

There is only one perfectionist, but you will become more like Christ

The wind beneath the kite is provided by our creator

Our skin may differ, but we shall love thy neighbor

We have been given favor, so let's return that seven times seven

Nonbelievers will perish while believers will rejoice in heaven

True Love

True love is refreshing, true love is engaging

True love is monogamous, true love is flagrant

True love is relentless, true love is honest

True love is painful, true love is bonding

True love is commitment, true love is open

True love is unbreakable, it can not be broken

True love is reliable, true love is envious

True love is venomous

True love is a blessing, true love is a curse

True love is refreshing, true love is birth

True love is crying, true love is laughing

True love is priceless, true love is everlasting

14

Thank God

Grey clouds and thunderstorms filled the skies, but thank God

My car won't start, so I have to take the bus to work, but thank God

My head is pounding and I'm sweating profusely, but thank God

I forgot my lunch on the kitchen counter, but thank God

They're assassinating my character, but thank God

They're talking about laying people off, but thank God

My wife just won't let me relax on my day off, but thank God

My tenant is late with the rent, but thank God

I have to take my son to basketball practice, but thank God

My wife wants to go on a cruise for our anniversary, but thank God

My daughter is engaged to be married, but thank God

Jesus

Being a believer doesn't exempt us from pain

Total strangers and the ones that we embrace are capable of injecting us with polarizing pain

Financial strain and carnal thoughts can pry open the flood gates to division

Therefore we must not only seek knowledge, but we must utilize our wisdom

It's bigger than me, it's bigger than all of us

Naysayers salivate at our blunders, so it's imperative that we exercise our trust

God said that he would never forsake us or give us more than we can bear

But sometimes we question his judgement and we throw up our hands and say this just isn't fair

But oh, no, we must stand up and display our resolve

Our mission is to praise him and spread the word, so we must remain involved

Jesus is the roman candle when the light bill is past due

He is the change in the sofa when there is no food

But the storm shall pass and the sun shall shine brighter than ever

Tears cascade down appreciative faces as we flourish in our endeavors

So, never settle-God wants us to prosper as much as possible

If we follow the light, we will overcome any and every obstacle

{Untitled, 2016}

Radiant rays from the sun pale in comparison to the light
that illuminates your soul

Your eyes are a best seller and your beauty is so bold

When life separated us, I prayed for this day

My prayers have been answered now I'm here to stay

Grey skies may appear and tears may fall

But our insurmountable love for each other and God will
enable us to conquer all

We crawled before we walked, now we're moving towards
success

I don't have to look too far to see how much I have been
blessed

You're truly a gift from God, I owe you my life and so much
more

Putting a smile on your face fuels my drive to push for more

You deserve the best and I want you to have everything
that your heart desires

I will dive into the ocean and I will walk through the fire

Because life without you is something that I refuse to
endure

Even though you've been through the storm, throughout it
your heart has remained pure

TMC

Some leave their environment with no intentions of returning

But your affinity for your community and your selflessness insured that your light won't stop burning

Many say you left too soon but that's definitely not the case

Music was unquestionably a catalyst, but your philanthropy is the reason no one will forget your face

This race is marathon you hit the nail on the head

Your interviews proved that in addition to being street smart you were well read

Your killer fled, lacking the capacity to process what he had just done

His emotions ignited his demons and he murdered one of God's sons'

Your body will perish but your spirit is forever present

We are celebrating your life around the world and enjoying your presents

I' praying for your family, I know God is filling their souls with directions

I know I speak for so many when I say that you are truly a blessing

{Excerpt 1}, No More Pain by Donnel Davis

Just beneath moonlit skies and commercial lighting, frantic footsteps rapped against patiently paved streets, which were inconveniently covered with a considerable amount of leftover rain. In an avid attempt to peer over his shoulder, this amateur runner lost his footing and inadvertently kissed the base of a meter reader. With no hesitation, he was back on his feet until he reached the parking garage where his rarified sedan awaited him. He craned his neck from side to side until he retrieved his keys from the pocket of his coffee colored pea coat and boarded his tinted machine.

The doors locked automatically, but a blanket of paranoia forced him to double-check what had become a standard feature. While he tried to track down his breath, his eyes darted from side to side like the anchor of the Bears' 85 defense. When he finally had come to the conclusion that he had successfully eluded the authorities and the "goody-good" civilians who were hot on his tail, his disturbed state was immediately erased and replaced with an impish grin.

A surge of empowerment raced through him as he embraced the godly deed that he had just performed. No blood found it's way on his impeccable garments. He had become a pro.

All the action had him parched, so he grabbed a bottled water from the back seat. When he turned around, his eyes were met with a glaring light of reflective chrome. The words that came from the mouth of the person holding the gun with an ironclad grip were loud and clear, but they fell on deaf ears.

{Excerpt 2}, No More Pain by Donnel Davis

In recent months, the nation had witnessed a significant spike in cemetery vandalism and unfortunately, Houston had not been excluded from his foolishness. Countless headstones had been extracted or sprayed with graffiti and trashcans overturned—a complete mess. Braylond closed his eyes and said a quick prayer in hopes that his parents' plot had been granted a gracious pass.

The sun had pushed its way through the morning sky when he saw the groundskeeper, Mr. Stoney, signal to him to him that visitation was set to begin. The town consensus was that the exaggerated limp that he displayed was the result of sleeping with a married man's wife...so rumor had it. The automated wrought iron gate opened like the mouth of Jaws and the vehicles passed through. After navigating the winding road for a half-mile, Braylond pulled into a parking spot.

He reached back and pulled out two Dr. Peppers and a bag of Doritos from the backseat of his tuxedo black 7 series BMW before he exited his pristine machine. He double-checked his pants pocket to make sure that he had the poem that he had penned for his parents. Braylond walked by countless headstones until he reached the two that read Mr. and Mrs. Foster. He was relieved to see that nothing had been tampered with. The grounds had been well manicured.

Without further ado, he squatted between the headstones and them a big hug. Texas-sized tears welled in his eyes before the laws of gravity took effect. This site was a safe haven. He was able to unharness his emotions without caution. It was safe to say that there were more than a few people who could relate to the pain that at times crippled him.

"Hi, mom. Hi, dad. It is a beautiful day. I wish that you two could be here to share all the success that I'm having. Graduation is right around the corner. Whoever thought that a kid from the bottom of Third Ward with two gangster-ass parents would be walking across the stage at such a prestigious university?"

He paused for a second.

"You did. I have befriended a couple people, but nobody really understands my struggle. Dad, I took after you. The girls are waiting in line the first of the month."

He let out an exaggerated chuckle.

Almost immediately after Braylond retrieved the poem from his pocket it started to pour down. With little hesitation, he sprinted towards his vehicle and climbed behind the wheel only to realize he'd dropped the poem.

"Damn, I can't keep up with that piece of paper!"

His frustration with himself was interrupted when a knock at the window startled him. In seconds his hands were wrapped around the handle of a revolver. Rather than looking for a victim, this stranger was instead holding the paper Braylond had lost.

"Here you go. I saw you drop this. I figured it might be pretty important. Have a blessed day."

Before Braylond could extend his gratitude, the stranger had disappeared into the heavy sheets of rain.